W9-BHR-329

ROCKFORD PUBLIC LIBRARY

3 1112 01621806 3

J 641.5945 GOU
Goulding, Sylvia
Italy

030209

WITHDRAWN

ROCKFORD PUBLIC LIBRARY

Rockford, Illinois

www.rockfordpubliclibrary.org

815-965-9511

FESTIVE FOODS
ITALY

Sylvia Goulding

CHELSEA
CLUBHOUSE

An Imprint of Chelsea House Publishers

ROCKFORD PUBLIC LIBRARY

Copyright © 2008 The Brown Reference Group plc.

All rights reserved. No part of this book may be reproduced or utilized in any form or by any means, electronic or mechanical, including photocopying, recording, or by any information storage and retrieval systems, without permission in writing from the publisher. For information contact:

Chelsea Clubhouse
An imprint of Chelsea House Publishers
132 West 31st Street
New York, NY 10001

Library of Congress Cataloging-in-Publication Data

Goulding, Sylvia.
  Festive foods / Sylvia Goulding. – 1st ed.
    v. cm.
  Includes bibliographical references and index.
  Contents: [1] China – [2] France – [3] Germany – [4] India – [5] Italy – [6] Japan – [7] Mexico – [8] United States.
  ISBN 978-0-7910-9751-9 (v. 1) – ISBN 978-0-7910-9752-6 (v. 2) – ISBN 978-0-7910-9756-4 (v. 3) – ISBN 978-0-7910-9757-1 (v. 4) – ISBN 978-0-7910-9753-3 (v. 5) – ISBN 978-0-7910-9754-0 (v. 6) – ISBN 978-0-7910-9755-7 (v. 7) – ISBN 978-0-7910-9758-8 (v. 8)
1. Cookery, International. 2. Gardening. 3. Manners and customs. I. Title.
  TX725.A1G56 2008
  641.59–dc22

                    2007042722

Chelsea Clubhouse books are available at special discounts when purchased in bulk quantities for businesses, associations, institutions, or sales promotions. Please call our Special Sales Department in New York at (212) 967-8800 or (800) 322-8755.

You can find Chelsea Clubhouse
on the World Wide Web at
http://www.chelseahouse.com

Printed and bound in Dubai

10 9 8 7 6 5 4 3 2 1

For The Brown Reference Group plc:
Project Editor: Sylvia Goulding
Cooking Editor: Angelika Ilies
Contributors: Carey Denton, Jacqueline Fortey, Sylvia Goulding
Photographers: Klaus Arras, Lucy Suleiman
Cartographer: Darren Awuah
Art Editor: Paula Keogh
Illustrator: Jo Gracie
Picture Researcher: Mike Goulding
Managing Editor: Bridget Giles
Production Director: Alastair Gourlay
Editorial Director: Lindsey Lowe
Children's Publisher: Anne O'Daly

Photographic Credits:
Front and Back Cover: Klaus Arras
Alamy: CuboImages srl 30, David Lyons 6, Stock Italia 29; **Fotolia:** 22, 32, 34, 40; **istock:** 12, 13, 16, 23, 30, 37, 38, 39; **Photolibrary:** Anthony Blake 28; **Shutterstock:** title page, 3, 4, 5, 7, 8, 9, 10, 13, 15, 20, 25, 31, 36, 42, 44, 45; **Stockfood:** Peter Eising 3, 27

With thanks to models:
Jamila, Mariam, Miho

Cooking Editor
Angelika Ilies has always been interested in cookery and other countries. She studied nutritional sciences in college. She has lived in the United States, England, and Germany. She has also traveled extensively and collected international recipes on her journeys. Angelika has written more than 70 cookbooks and cooking card series. She currently lives in Frankfurt, Germany, with her two children and has spent much time researching children's nutrition. Both children regularly cook with their mother.

To be carried out safely, many of the recipes in this book require adult supervision and assistance. While rules and safety precautions have been noted throughout the book, readers are reminded always to use caution when cooking, using sharp tools, or lighting fires. The publisher, editors, and authors have made every reasonable effort to ensure that the recipes in this book are safe when followed as instructed but assume no responsibility for any damage caused or sustained while carrying out the recipes in the book. The recipes and ingredients recommended for the dishes contained in this book are aimed at healthy individuals and are not specific to any individuals or their particular circumstances. Always check the list of ingredients for each specific dish. If you are in any doubt as to whether an ingredient is inappropriate for you, you should consult your physician. Do not use any ingredients that you may be allergic to (or think you may have an allergy to).

Contents

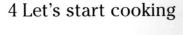

let's
START COOKING

Cooking is fun—you learn about different ingredients and cooking methods, you find out how things taste, and you can serve to your family and friends a meal that you have cooked yourself! Some of the recipes in this book have steps that need adult help—ask a parent or other adult if they will be your kitchen assistant while you cook a meal.

This line tells you how many people the meal will feed.

In this box, you find out which ingredients you need for your meal.

WHAT YOU NEED:

SERVES 4 PEOPLE:

2¼ cups white rice
4 eggs, beaten
light soy sauce
4 tablespoons
    groundnut or
    soy oil
2 green onions
⅓ cup peeled shrimps
⅓ cup ham
⅓ cup green peas

Check before you start that you have everything at home. If something is missing, write it on your shopping list. Get all the ingredients ready before you start cooking.

◁ The kitchen job I like best is going to the markets and choosing food for dinner. I always buy the freshest that I can find, from local farmers.

! WHEN TO GET help

Most cooking involves cutting ingredients and heating them in some way, whether frying, boiling, or cooking in the oven. Each time you see this exclamation mark, be extra careful as you cook and make sure your adult kitchen assistant is around to help.

For many meals you need to chop an onion. First cut off a thin slice at both ends. Pull off the peel. Cut the onion in half from end to end. Put one half with the cut side down on the chopping board. Hold it with one hand and cut end-to-end slices with the other hand. Hold the slices together and cut across the slices to make small cubes. Make sure you do not cut yourself!

Other recipes in this book use fresh garlic. Break a whole head of garlic into separate cloves. Cut the top and the bottom off each clove, and pull off the papery skin. Now you can either chop the garlic clove with a sharp knife, or you can use a garlic crusher to squeeze the garlic directly into the skillet or saucepan. If you are worried about garlic breath, chew some parsley.

With a **pasta machine** you can roll out long thin strands of pasta for spaghetti, or wider ones for tagliatelle.

Parmesan graters allow you to grate the cheese directly onto the meal. The grater prevents the cheese flying around.

Pepper mills are a useful tool to have in any kitchen, because pepper tastes much better when it is freshly grated.

With a **spaghetti spoon** you can scoop up and serve pasta. The prongs prevent the pasta from slipping off the spoon.

A trip around
ITALY

Italy is famous for its long history, art, opera, fashion, and its Mediterranean beaches, but it is best-loved for its food. Pasta and pizza have conquered the world.

Italy is a country in southern Europe just a little larger than Arizona. Its northern border runs along the Dolomite mountains, which are part of the Alps. France, Switzerland, Austria, and Slovenia are Italy's neighbors to the north and west.

Most of the Italian mainland is a peninsula— it is surrounded by water on three sides. Italy forms the shape of a boot with a high heel. It looks like it is about to kick the large island of Sicily. Sardinia is an island to the west. It is separated from the mainland by the Tyrrhenian Sea. The Apennine mountain range runs from north to south down the center of Italy for 870 miles.

Rome is the Italian capital. Rome has just over 2½ million inhabitants. Other large cities are Milan, Naples, Turin, Palermo, Genoa, Bologna, and Florence.

The north

The far north of Italy has spectacular scenery. There are Alpine peaks, forests of beech, oak, and chestnut trees, and sparkling lakes. The largest lakes are Lake Garda, Lake Maggiore, and

◁ *About 58 million Italians* live mainly in the large cities, such as Rome, Naples, and Milan. They speak Italian, and most are Roman Catholic in religion.

◁ *Italy* is a country in southern Europe. It sits in the middle of the Mediterranean Sea. It shares borders with France, Switzerland, Austria, and Slovenia.

1 ◁ *The Dolomites* are a majestic mountain range in northern Italy. People ski here in winter and hike in summer. In some areas people speak German.

△ *The Vatican* is a tiny, independent country, right in the middle of the Italian capital Rome. It is home to the Pope and the center of the Roman Catholic Church. St. Peter's Square and Basilica *(above)* are its most famous sights.

▽ *Pompeii* was a thriving city in the ancient Roman Empire. In the year AD 79, Mt. Vesuvius erupted. This volcano buried the city under thick layers of ash. It has now been uncovered.

▷ *The beautiful coastline* south of Naples and the small island of Capri have attractive bays with rocks, sunny beaches, colorful fishing villages, and steep, rugged hillsides.

NORTH AMERICA · ASIA · EUROPE · ITALY · AFRICA

GERMANY · CZECH REPUBLIC · FRANCE · SLOVAKIA · AUSTRIA · HUNGARY · SWITZERLAND · Alps · SLOVENIA · CROATIA · BOSNIA-HERZEGOVINA · SERBIA AND MONTENEGRO · ALBANIA · GREECE

Milan · Po River · Venice · Bologna · Florence · Ligurian Sea · ITALY · ROME · Adriatic Sea · Corsica · Sardinia · Naples · Bari · Pompeii · Tyrrhenian Sea · SICILY · Catania · MEDITERRANEAN SEA

Lake Como, which is one of the deepest in Europe. Farther south, the Po River flows from west to east across the fertile North Italian Plain. Most of the country's industry and agriculture are based here. The Po River flows into the sea on the east coast, south of Venice. It forms a delta (river mouth) with mudflats and lagoons (shallow inland seas).

The winters are very cold in the Italian Alps, with heavy snowfalls. The snow attracts skiers and snowboarders from around the world. Winter can also be cold and foggy in the Po Valley. There is generally more rain in northern Italy than in the south, and the summers are warm.

Central Italy

The Arno River flows westward from the Apennine mountains into the Tyrrhenian Sea. It passes through the historic cities of Florence and Pisa. The Tiber River also rises in the mountains. It flows southward through the

▽ *Manarola is one of the Cinque Terre*, or Five Cities, in Liguria. The cities could once only be reached by sea, on footpaths, or on mule tracks. Today, the beautiful cities and the rugged cliffs to which they cling have been declared a World Heritage site.

beautiful regions of Tuscany and Umbria to the sea. Many tourists are attracted to the beautiful countryside here.

The city of Rome was founded on the Tiber's eastern banks nearly 3,000 years ago. The ancient Roman Empire started from here and spread across much of Europe.

The wild, hilly landscape of the Abruzzi region in the east includes many spectacular national parks. Brown bears, lynxes, and wolves still roam in the remote areas; these animals are protected by laws.

The Marche region north of the Abruzzi has rolling countryside and attractive hilltop towns. Parts of the east coast are fringed with long sandy beaches. High areas in central Italy are colder and wetter than on the coast.

The south

The warm, dry south of Italy is home to two of Europe's most famous volcanoes. Mt. Vesuvius (4,202 feet) overlooks the city

△ **Single farms** are dotted around Tuscany's beautiful, soft, rolling hills with their scattered olive trees and cypresses. The capital of this region is Florence, one of the world's most important cities for art. Tuscany is also famous for its well-preserved medieval villages.

of Naples on the west coast. Mt. Etna (10,910 feet) is Europe's tallest volcano. It rises above the town of Taormina on Sicily. From time to time, Etna erupts and sends hot lava streams over its surroundings. Some eruptions are so dangerous that people leave their villages.

Calabria, the peninsula that forms Italy's "toe," is rugged and mountainous. It is surrounded by beautiful blue seas. There are vineyards and orchards on its lower slopes, and forests and bare highlands on higher ground. Puglia is a flatter region at the "heel" of Italy. It is known for its wine and olive oil. People in southern Italy are generally much poorer than in the north.

The food we grow in
ITALY

With its long coastlines, mountains and hills, plains and rivers, Italy is perfectly placed to grow delicious food.

*T*he Mediterranean diet is thought to be one of the healthiest of all diets. Its main ingredients are olive oil, tomatoes, garlic, fresh fruits and vegetables, and lots of fish. All these are grown, caught, or made in Italy.

The North Italian Plain

The flat, fertile Po Valley is Italy's richest agricultural region. Farmers raise cattle for milk and cheese, and keep pigs. They grow corn, rice, wheat, sugarbeet, fruit, and vegetables. Corn is ground into cornmeal, and this is boiled to make a popular dish, called *polenta*. A short-grain rice that is grown here is made into delicious *risotto*.

Grapes are cultivated for wine, but the winters in the north are too cold for growing olives. The area around the town of Parma is the center for delicious Parmesan cheese and Parma ham, known as *prosciutto*. The city of Bologna is also renowned for good food and for its *bolognese* meat sauce. It is the capital of the Emilia-Romagna region, one of Italy's main areas for raising animals and growing cereals, fruit, and vegetables.

MOSTLY MUSHROOMS

In Italy, mushroom hunting is a hobby. People learn from their parents which mushrooms can be eaten and which cannot. Even so, about 40,000 people in Italy suffer from mushroom poisoning each year.

Mountains and forests

In the pretty small villages of the Dolomites in the north, people move their cows to high meadows for the summer. Meanwhile, they grow crops and cut hay in the winter pastures. Farmers in northern Italy also grow fruits, such as apples, and vegetables.

Large areas of the Apennine mountains in the center are covered with forests. The lower slopes have been cleared for farmland. Cattle, sheep, and goats graze here. There are groves of sweet chestnut trees on many hillsides in northern and central Italy.

In the fall, Italians go into the woods with baskets on their arms to gather *porcini* and other wild mushrooms. Mushrooms are sold fresh, dried, or bottled in oil.

White truffles are highly prized. They grow in northwestern Italy around Alba and in the center around Rieti. Specially trained dogs or pigs sniff out these mushrooms underground.

◁ **Goats are raised** in the upland pastures and in the south of Italy. They yield goats' milk, which is made into cheese. Italians also like eating the meat of young goats, or kids.

Central Italy

The uplands and plains west of the Apennine mountains are among Italy's most important agricultural regions. This central area has a Mediterranean climate, with hot summers and mild winters. It is ideal for growing grapes, olives, and wheat. Olives are pressed to make olive oil, and wheat flour is used to make pasta and bread.

Each Italian region has its own favorite pasta sauce. Pesto is made from basil leaves; basil is grown around Genoa and in Tuscany. Bolognese sauce comes from the meat-raising area around Bologna. Naples is famous for its tomato sauces, often called *napolitana*, and *siciliana* is a spicy tomato sauce from the island of Sicily in southern Italy.

Farmers in Central Italy also keep animals. On the hills of Tuscany, excellent grain, olives, and beans are grown. Famous products from here are olive oil and salamis, and a well-known dish is Tuscan bean soup.

A speciality on the mountainous island of Sardinia is hard Pecorino cheese. It is made from sheep's milk. The Abruzzo region in the western part of the center is known for its lamb and pork dishes, and smoked cheeses.

▽ **Olive trees** grow best where they are safe from frost. The trees can get very gnarled. The fruits are often picked by hand. They are pressed to make olive oil—the best is unfiltered oil from the first cold pressing.

Southern Italy

Farmers in the south rear cattle, buffalo, sheep, and goats. Buffalo milk is used to make mozzarella cheese. This cheese is an important ingredient in many pizza dishes. All the famous Mediterranean vegetables, including tomatoes, eggplant, bell peppers, and zucchini, grow well here.

Off the coast of Puglia, fishermen catch octopus, shrimps, scallops, and oysters for seafood dishes. Sicilians enjoy swordfish, snapper, and cuttlefish.

Sicily is also famous for its citrus fruit. The lemons that grow here are enormous and very juicy. Sheep and goats are also kept on Sicily. Tasty desserts are made with ricotta cheese, which is made from sheep's milk.

◁ **Fresh fish** is available at all Italian markets. People buy it in the morning, when the boats have come in from the sea. They eat the fish on the same day. It is often grilled and served with a squeeze of lemon and some bread.

CELEBRITY TRUFFLE

A giant white truffle the size of a small handbag was sold at an auction in London in 2005. The mystery bidder paid 92,000 euros ($124,573) for it. The truffle had been found by trained truffle hounds under an oak tree in Alba, in the Piedmont region.

let's make...
MINESTRONE

This recipe is from Liguria. My grandparents grow all the vegetables for minestrone in their own yard. Grandma calls this soup "vitamin soup" because it is so full of goodness.

WHAT YOU NEED:

SERVES 4 PEOPLE:

9 ounces waxy potatoes

about 2 pounds mixed
   vegetables (for example
   broad beans, French
   beans, kidney beans,
   fennel, carrots, leeks,
   broccoli, zucchini)

10 ounces tomatoes

1 onion

3 ounces pancetta (smoked
   bacon); meat is optional

2 tablespoons olive oil

1 garlic clove

2 pints vegetable stock

½ bunch flat-leaf parsley

1½ bunch basil

salt, black pepper

soup noodles

4 tablespoons pesto (home-made or from the jar)

2 ounces Pecorino or Parmesan cheese

◁ Broccoli, tomatoes, and potatoes are my favorites. I have also made this soup with frozen vegetables, but Grandma says that's cheating.

WHAT'S THIS: pancetta?

Pancetta is an Italian bacon. It is made from the belly of a pig, and is usually sold rolled. If you cannot find it, use an unsmoked bacon instead. If you prefer to make meat-free minestrone, though, just leave the pancetta out.

1 Peel then wash the potatoes and cut them into small cubes. Wash and trim the other vegetables. Also cut them into small cubes. Put the tomatoes into a small bowl, pour hot water over them, and allow to stand for 1 minute.

2 Pull off the tomato skins. Halve and deseed the tomatoes. Cut out the stems and throw them away. Cube the tomato flesh. Peel and chop the onion *(see page 5)*. Cube the pancetta.

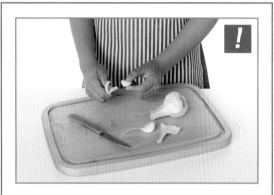

3 Heat the oil in a saucepan. Add the pancetta and fry until the fat starts to run. Add the onions. Fry and stir from time to time, until the onions turn golden yellow. Don't let them burn.

4 Peel the garlic and press it into the saucepan *(see page 5)*. Add all the vegetables, apart from the tomatoes. Fry for 2–3 minutes and stir from time to time. Pour in the stock and bring to a boil. Stir in the tomatoes. Turn the heat to low, add the soup noodles, and simmer the soup for about 20 minutes.

5 Chop the herbs and stir them into the minestrone. Season the soup with salt and pepper. Ladle it into individual bowls and serve with pesto and freshly grated cheese.

let's make...
PASTA SAUCES

Here are two recipes for pasta sauces—one is cold, and one is hot. You can eat both sauces with different shaped pasta, but spaghetti works well with both.

▽ Do you like pasta? What a question! I could eat it every single day. Luckily, Mom has a zillion pasta sauce recipes.

WHAT YOU NEED:

TO MAKE PESTO:

2 ounces pine nuts
3 or 4 handfuls basil (about 3 ounces)
3 garlic cloves
salt, black pepper

7 tablespoons cold-pressed olive oil
2 ounces Parmesan cheese

TO MAKE BOLOGNESE SAUCE:

3 ounces smoked bacon
1 onion
1 garlic clove
1 carrot
1 stick celery
3 tablespoons olive oil
1 lb ground beef

2 tablespoons chopped parsley
1 pinch ground cloves
salt and black pepper
2 cups stock
1½ lbs canned tomatoes (peeled and chopped)

WHAT'S THIS: _al dente?_

In many recipes it says, cook the pasta until "al dente." Pasta tastes best, if it still has some "bite." This means, it is not hard, but also not soggy and limp. It's not easy to stop at the right stage of cooking. Fish out one strand of spaghetti, quickly refresh it under cold water, and taste it to check.

1 **To make the pesto:**
Brown the pine nuts in a skillet without fat. Stir them until they start to brown. Take them out immediately. Pull the leaves off the basil. Peel the garlic. !

2 With a handheld blender or a mixer, purée all the ingredients to make a smooth paste. Serve the pesto cold.

3 **To make the bolognese sauce:**
Cube the bacon. Peel the onion and the garlic and chop both. Scrape the carrot clean, trim the celery stick. Cube carrot and celery.

4 Heat the oil in a large saucepan. Add the bacon, onion, garlic, carrot, and celery, and fry for 5 minutes. Stir from time to time. !

5 Add the ground beef. Break up any clumps and fry until the meat has turned brown. Add the parsley, cloves, salt, and pepper and stir. Pour in the stock. Add the tomatoes and stir to combine. Bring back to a boil, then turn the heat to low. Cover the saucepan and allow to simmer for at least 3 hours. !

6 Stir from time to time. If the sauce seems too thick, add a little more stock. Serve hot.

let's make...
TOMATO RISOTTO

Risotto is a north Italian dish as this is where most of the rice is grown. There are many recipes: in Milan, people add saffron, and around Venice people use the ink of cuttlefish!

▽ Risotto goes well with most ingredients. Aside from tomatoes, you could also try it with mushrooms, herbs, or different cheeses.

WHAT YOU NEED:

TO SERVE 4 PEOPLE:

1 onion
1 tablespoon butter
3 tablespoons olive oil
9 ounces risotto rice
2¾ cups stock
4 ounces sundried tomatoes in oil
1 large bunch mixed herbs
2 tablespoons pine nuts
salt, black pepper
4 tablespoons freshly grated Pecorino cheese

WHAT'S THIS: risotto rice?

To make risotto, choose Arborio, Carnaroli, or Vialone rice. All these rice have big, short, round grains, and they can soak up plenty of liquid.

MY TIP

Don't wash the rice before cooking—it washes out the starch, which gives it texture.

1 Peel and chop the onion *(see page 5)*. In a saucepan, heat the butter and the olive oil. When it starts to foam, add the onion. Fry and stir for about 3 minutes, until the onion is transparent (looks glassy).

2 Add the rice and stir until all the grains are covered with oil.

3 Pour in the stock, a small amount at a time. Each time, stir and cook until the stock has been absorbed (the mixture starts to look dry). Add more stock and continue.

4 Meanwhile, finely chop the sundried tomatoes. Wash the herbs and shake them dry. Throw away any yellow leaves and thick stems, and roughly chop the leaves.

6 Stir the tomatoes and herbs into the rice, when it is nearly done. Season with salt and pepper, stir, and cook for a few minutes more. The risotto should be just moist—neither dry, nor sloppy. Sprinkle it with the pine nuts and grated cheese. Serve.

5 Heat a skillet without oil. Add the pine nuts. Roast them, stirring all the time. Take them off the heat as soon as they start to turn brown.

How we celebrate in
ITALY

Italy celebrates twelve national holidays each year, and there are many more regional and local holidays to enjoy.

I n Italy, the special days in the Christian calendar are marked by big festivals. The harvest of particular local foods is also a good reason to party, and of course there is always a saint's day to celebrate.

Carnival

Carnival, the time before the fasting in Lent, is celebrated in many different towns in Italy. The most famous is the masked carnival of Venice—the city that has many more canals than roads. The first record of a carnival in Venice dates from 1268. The greatest novelty then was the fact that people wore masks.

Nowadays, tourists from all over the world flock to Venice to watch and to join in. The carnival starts with the "Flight of the Angel." A tightrope walker walks from St. Mark's Bell Tower to the seat of the Doge (the governor). Many different closing events happen on the last day, "martedi grasso" or Shrove Tuesday (Mardi Gras). In the seaside town of Viareggio in Tuscany, for example, people wear costumes and don giant papier mâché heads as they parade through the town.

Easter

After a period of fasting, people celebrate Easter. This starts on Good Friday when the bells stop ringing to remember the death of Christ. They start ringing again on Easter Sunday, when Jesus rose from the dead. People hug and kiss each other. They wish each other *Buon Pasqua*, "Happy Easter." In Florence, Easter starts with a loud bang, "the explosion of the cart." There are also many Easter parades in Italian cities.

Eggs are an important part of the Easter festivities. They symbolize life, fertility, and renewal. Children search for nests with Easter eggs. The eggs are painted in colors or made from chocolate. The other important Easter food is roast lamb. The lamb symbolizes Jesus and the good shepherd.

◁ **The best masks** in the Venice carnival can be seen in St. Mark's Square. But it is hard to get to the square and to find a space there—the start of Carnivale now regularly attracts about 120,000 people!

NAME THE FRITTER

For Carnival, people eat fritters that have many different strange names. They are known as cenci (tatters), donzelli (young ladies), lattughe (lettuce), nastri delle suore (nuns' ribbons), crostoli (crusts), and chiacchere (gossip).

Christmas

Christmas celebrations in Italy start in early December and continue until Epiphany on January 6. Before Christmas, beautiful nativity scenes are on show. The first crib was made for Saint Francis of Assisi in the thirteenth century. Many old cribs contain detailed figures carved out of wood. They wear beautiful clothes of precious fabrics.

Italians eat their main Christmas meal on Christmas Eve. What they eat varies from region to region, and from family to family.

△ **Nativity scenes** can be seen everywhere in Italy. Cribs from Naples are especially famous. Some take up several rooms and include many life-size figures.

◁ *The Cheese Festival* in Bra, northern Italy, is celebrated in September. Stalls line the street with cheeses for people to try. It is one of many Italian food festivals. Other festivals celebrate mushrooms, melons, sweet chestnuts, or pizza.

Often the Christmas meal features fish, seafood, and many vegetables but no meat. But one thing that all Italians eat is *panettone*, a light, spongelike cake with candied fruits.

La Befana

Today, many families exchange their gifts on Christmas Eve, but traditionally this was done on January 6, or Three Kings' Day.

Italian legend tells that on their way to see the baby Jesus the three kings met La Befana. This kind old woman told them the way. She was busy, but she followed the kings later with her broom. Unfortunately she never found the baby Jesus and so she is still searching today. Every January 6, she travels around on her broomstick and puts gifts and candies into the stockings that children leave out for her.

let's make...
ROAST LAMB

This is a very festive dish, and we all look forward to eating it. We often serve lamb at Easter, when all the family come to visit. If the weather is nice, we eat outside.

▽ This is a labor-saving dish. The meal comes out all in one—meat, potatoes, vegetables, and gravy.

WHAT YOU NEED:

SERVES 4 TO 6 PEOPLE:

1 small leg of lamb (about 3½ lbs)
4 garlic cloves
6 tablespoons olive oil
salt, black pepper
2–3 tablespoons fresh thyme leaves
1½ lbs new potatoes
1½ lbs zucchini
2 red bell peppers
2 yellow bell peppers
2 large onions
3½ cups stock

WHAT SORT OF lamb?

For really special occasions we buy *abbacchio*. This is very young baby lamb, and it is sold whole. It is very tender and has virtually no fat.

MY TIP

This recipe also works well if you replace the lamb with kid—that's a baby goat!

1 Heat the oven to 480°F. Wash the lamb and pat it dry with paper towels. Peel the garlic *(see page 5)* and cut each clove into thin slivers.

2 Make cuts in the meat and stuff a garlic sliver into each one. Wash the thyme, pull the leaves off the stems, and chop them. In a small bowl, combine the oil, salt, pepper, and thyme. Rub the mixture all over the lamb's skin.

3 Place the lamb onto a deep baking tray. Roast it in the oven for about 20 minutes.

4 Wearing gloves, pull out the tray, and pour half the stock into the bottom of the tray. Reduce the heat to 400°F. Return the lamb to the oven and cook for another 40 minutes.

5 Peel and wash the potatoes. Peel the onions. Wash and trim the zucchini. Wash, trim, and deseed the bell peppers. Cut all the vegetables into cubes, strips, or chunks. Arrange them in the tray around the lamb.

6 Pour in the rest of the stock. Put the tray back in the oven and cook the lamb for another 60 minutes. After 30 minutes, take out the tray and turn the vegetables with a wooden spatula.

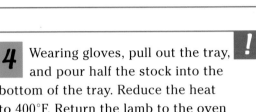

let's make...
PANETTONE

For Christmas my Mom always bakes panettone. She competes with my aunts to see who can make the biggest, lightest, airiest, prettiest.... I don't care, as long as I can have a piece (or two)!

WHAT YOU NEED:

TO MAKE 8-10 PIECES OF CAKE:

1 cube fresh yeast (2 ounces)
⅔ cup lukewarm milk
1 teaspoon sugar
14 ounces plain flour
5 egg yolks
1 pinch salt
⅔ cup softened butter
⅔ cup dried fruits (raisins, dates, figs, candied lemon or orange zest)
⅝ cup chopped almonds (optional)

PLUS:

butter for greasing and flour
for the mold
1 egg yolk
a few candied fruits
confectioner's sugar

◁ Sometimes we go skiing in the Dolomites for Christmas— and we take panettone with us. As if you couldn't buy it up there!

WHAT MAKES THE CAKE SO LIGHT?

In traditional recipes, the dough for this cake has to rise three times. It takes several days to make a panettone. This process is called proofing. It ensures that the cake is light. Our version is a faster way to bake it, but it tastes just as delicious.

1 Crumble the yeast into a bowl. Add a little milk and stir until smooth. Stir in the sugar and a bit of flour. Cover the bowl with a clean cloth. Leave it for a few minutes.

2 In a large bowl, combine the yeast mixture with the rest of the milk and flour, the egg yolks, salt, and the butter. Knead everything with clean hands until you have a smooth dough. Cover the dough with a cloth and allow it to rest in a warm place for 1 hour.

4 Heat the oven to 400°F. Chop the dried fruits. Knead the fruits and almonds into the dough. Put the dough into the mold. Cover it with a cloth and allow it to rise for at least 30 minutes. **!**

3 Fit a ring of aluminum foil around the inside of a large loose-bottom baking tin (7 to 8 inches) so the edge stands higher than the mold. Put some softened butter on a paper towel. Rub this over the inside of the mold and foil to grease. Dust both with a little flour.

5 Bake the cake on the lowest shelf for 45 minutes, until it is golden brown. Take it out of the oven, but allow it to cool in the mold for 20 minutes. Gently lift it out of the mold. Place it on a rack, cover with a cloth, and allow to cool completely. **!**

6 Decorate the cake with candied fruits. Put the confectioner's sugar into a small sieve and shake it above the cake to dust it. Serve and enjoy!

How we celebrate at home in
ITALY

In Italy people celebrate their personal occasions, such as a birthdays, jubilees, or weddings, together with the entire family, all the neighbors, and the village priest. In fact, most people in the village join in. This is what happens in the countryside. Of course it is not possible in the large cities.

▽ *Family banquets* for special occasions such as weddings often take place in people's own homes. Long tables and benches are set out in the yard and covered with white tablecloths. Everyone joins in. The meals often last for many hours, and the dancing and music continue through the night.

Birthdays and name days

Traditionally, Italian children celebrate their birthdays and their name days. Until recently, all children in Italy were named after a saint. Often babies are named after the saint on whose day they were born. Most Italians are Catholics, and the Catholic Church names at least one saint on each day of the year. In the past, the name day was more important than the birthday. But today more Italians celebrate the day on which they were born. The older the child, the more painful the birthday—on their birthdays, Italian children traditionally have their ears pulled as many times as they are years old!

△ **Confetti** is often thrown at a newlywed couple. But another sort of confetti—almond candies—are also handed out to groom, bride, and wedding guests. These sweet favors are said to sweeten the couple's life.

SHATTERED

In some parts of Italy, the bride and groom symbolically shatter a glass after their wedding—the glass shards are said to represent the years of happiness they will enjoy in their married life.

29

◁ **The middle of the town square** may be used for special celebrations. Tables are set out in front of the church where the mass is said. The good weather allows people to enjoy the meal outdoors and dance through the night.

Cakes and pastries

The wedding cake is a multilayered tower of sponge cakes. Each layer is smaller than the one below. The cake is covered in soft, white cream icing. On top stand miniature models of a smiling bride and groom.

A *cassata* is a special dessert cake that people often eat at family events. Another traditional wedding pastry is called *wanda*. These are shaped like bowties and wish the couple good fortune.

Weddings

When the bride and groom arrive at the church, they have to pass under a bowed ribbon that is draped across the doorway. It symbolizes that the couple are about to "tie the knot."

After the wedding, the guests make their way to the restaurant or the bride's home, where the party is celebrated. Everyone goes by car and sounds their car horns so that all bystanders find out about the happy event.

▷ **The wedding cake** has models of two miniature people on top: the bridegroom and the bride. The cake is made from the finest ingredients. After the wedding meal, the couple slice the cake, and every guest eats a slice of cake with their coffee.

Italian confetti

In Italy, confetti are not the paper confetti thrown at weddings—these are called *coriandoli* in Italian. Instead, Italian confetti are sugared almond favors. At special occasions, for example at christenings, first communions, weddings, and special anniversaries, all the guests receive confetti. The almonds are wrapped in tulle (a starched net fabric) and decorated with ribbons. They come in colors. At christenings, the almonds are colored pale blue for a baby boy and pink for a baby girl. The confetti are white for communions and weddings; and they are silver and red in color for anniversaries and jubilees.

Village celebrations

Every town and small village in Italy has its own patron saint. This day is a local holiday. It is celebrated with a mass in church. Afterward there are processions, fun fairs, village banquets, music, and dances.

People come from near and far. Those who are on vacation and others who have second homes in the area happily join in the local events. It is a time to meet with family and old friends and to share a laugh over a meal.

◁ **A carved watermelon** is a special table decoration for an event such as birthdays, christenings, or jubilees. This melon has two turtledoves carved into the skin. Others may have the name of the celebrant on it.

SWEET INDIGESTION

In 1501, at the wedding banquet of Lucrezia Borgia and Alfonso D'Este, the Duke of Ferrara, the guests ate more than 260 pounds of confetti! That's more than the normal weight of a grown man.

RECIPE: Saltimbocca

let's make...
SALTIMBOCCA

The name of this dish makes me laugh: *salt-im-bocca* means "leap-in-the-mouth." And this dish is so delicious, it just jumps off the plate and directly into your mouth!

WHAT YOU NEED:

SERVES 4 PEOPLE:

8 thin slices of veal
  cutlets or scallops
  (weighing about
  1 lb 2 ounces
  in total)
white pepper
8 very thin slices
  of Parma ham
2 sprigs of sage
2 tablespoons butter
  or olive oil
salt
½ cup vegetable stock
sage leaves and lemon
  wedges to garnish

◁ You can make this dish with pork or chicken or cutlets too, but do take out the toothpick!

WHAT'S THIS: sage?

Sage is a kitchen herb with gray-green, fuzzy leaves. When you buy them, choose leaves that have no spots, and that aren't starting to curl up.

MY TIP

Cover leftover sage with olive oil, and it'll keep in the fridge for 2 months.

1 Lay the veal cutlets onto the work surface. Tap them with a meat mallet or the back of a knife to flatten. Grind white pepper over the meat.

2 Place one slice of Parma ham on each veal cutlet. Wash and pat dry the sage. Pull off the leaves. Place one leaf on top of each ham slice.

3 Use small wooden sticks or toothpicks to pin the sage and the ham to the veal cutlets.

4 Put the butter or oil in a large skillet and heat until it starts to foam. Place the cutlets in the pan and fry them for about 2 minutes, until they are lightly browned. Turn them over and fry for another 2 minutes. **!**

5 Season the cutlets with salt. Place them on a serving platter. Cover the platter with aluminum foil and keep it warm in the oven (at 200°F). **!**

6 Pour the stock into the pan. Stir with a wooden spoon to loosen the brown bits. Taste-test, and add more salt or pepper if needed. Serve the sauce with the cutlets. **!**

let's make...
CASSATA

This is not an ice cream but a delicious cake that we eat as a festive dessert. The original Arabic recipe was introduced to Sicily around a thousand years ago.

▽ This cake is so good, you'd want there to be a family party every day of the year! The only problem: you look away once, and the cake is gone! (Little brother!)

WHAT YOU NEED:

TO MAKE 1 CASSATA:

4 ounces bitter chocolate
10–14 ounces mixed candied fruits
5 ounces sugar
5 drops vanilla
juice of ½ orange
1¾ lbs ricotta cheese
1 round, three-layer sponge cake (9–10 inches diameter)
½ lb whipping cream

WHAT'S THIS: candied fruit?

Candied fruit is, in fact, crystallized. It is a method of preserving the fruit, so it can be kept for longer. When just ripe, the fruit is dipped into hot sugar syrup. This is repeated with ever stronger syrups until all the water in the fruit has been replaced by the sugar.

Finely chop the chocolate with a sharp knife. Also chop about 5 ounces of the candied fruits.

2 Put the sugar and 7 tablespoons water into a small saucepan, and bring to a boil, stirring all the time. Over medium heat, continue cooking and stirring until the mixture turns into a light syrup. Take the pan off the heat. Stir in the vanilla and the orange juice. Allow to cool a little.

4 Place one sponge cake on a platter. Fasten the cake ring around the base. With a spoon, spread half the cream on top, then cover with a second sponge cake. Spread the rest of the cream on top and cover with the last sponge cake. Put the cake into the fridge to set for at least 3 hours.

3 In a large bowl, beat the ricotta cheese with a wooden spoon until it is creamy. Stir in the sugar syrup. Then add the chopped chocolate and fruits, and stir to combine well.

5 Take off the cake ring. Whisk the whipping cream with a handheld whisk until it is stiff. With a plastic spatula, spread the whipped cream over the top and the sides of the cassata. Arrange the candied fruits in a pattern on top and serve.

How we live in
ITALY

More Italians live in towns and cities than in the countryside. Industry and commerce are concentrated in the north. In the south, more people work in agriculture.

How people live

In the towns and cities, most families live in apartments rather than in houses. Many old houses in the city centers have been turned into elegant and expensive apartments. But in the suburbs of the large cities, most people live in modern tall apartment blocks. Large areas are given over to such apartment buildings. In the countryside and in small villages, people live in one-family homes.

Italy's population has not increased since the 1980s. Many families have only one child. Most young people live at home until they are ready to get married. Their parents often help them buy or rent an apartment in the same block or at least nearby.

▽ **In the cities**, people live in apartments. Some areas have many such blocks crammed together.

△ *In the country*, some people still travel by horse and cart. Not all houses have heating, and the toilets may be outside. But young Italians also use mobile phones, own computers, play video games, and listen to their i-Pods.

VACATIONS

Three in four Italians vacation in their own country. Most escape from the heat of the cities to the seaside resorts, while some go to the mountains. They mostly vacation in the month of August, when schools and factories close.

Lunch and riposo

Everything stops at lunchtime in Italy. Offices, shops, and schools close. Most people eat lunch at home with their families. Lunch is the main meal of the day. Normally, people eat at least two courses: a pasta dish, known as *primo piatto*, followed by a meat or fish dish, the *secundo piatto*, served with salad or vegetables. On hot summer days, *antipasti*, a selection of cold meats, seafood, and vegetables are a popular choice.

After lunch everyone rests. This is known as the *riposo*. Shops and offices do not open again until at least 4 P.M., so there is time for everyone to sleep. It is not considered polite to visit, or even phone, anyone between 2 P.M. and 4 P.M. in the afternoon. Children

have to stay indoors so that they don't disturb others with their noisy games. But modern business is changing this custom. Today many people can only take a short break.

Pastimes

Italians are sociable people. One of their favorite pastimes is simply to stroll around their town or neighborhood. This is so popular there is a name for it, the *passeggiata*. Italians also like

to look good, so everyone dresses up for the occasion. In summer it is often so hot during the day that people wait until dusk to go out. Children often play outside at 10 P.M. or later.

Soccer is a huge passion in Italy. The big matches are played on Sunday afternoon and many people go to watch and support their local team. But Italians also love to play soccer, to watch matches on TV together, and to talk about it endlessly. Other popular sports are baseball, horseback riding, and cycling.

Italians love food. They enjoy eating out. Families visit the pizzeria, where the food is cooked in an open wood-burning stove. In the summer, the local *gelateria*, or ice-cream parlor, is a favorite meeting place.

▽ **Pizzerias** and ice-cream parlors are very popular places for family parties. They are also gathering points for young people, much as in the United States and elsewhere.

Going to School

Children start school when they are six years old. They attend elementary school until the age of eleven, and then they go to middle school until they are fourteen. After that they go to high school for four or five years.

Students can choose between technical schools, science, classical, teacher training, and language schools. Children go to school six days a week. The school day starts early, at 8.30 A.M., and finishes at about 1 P.M. Pupils work straight through, then they go home for lunch and the afternoon *riposo*.

CONE-GRATULATIONS!

An ice-cream vendor, Italo Marchioni, who emigrated from Italy to New York, invented the ice-cream cone in 1896.

let's make...
ANTIPASTI

Antipasti means "before the pasta," as it is the course we eat before the pasta course. Marinated peppers are one of many dishes you can serve as a starter.

▽ I like to arrange different antipasti on my plate so they make a picture. Do you like this clown's face?

WHAT YOU NEED:

SERVES 4 PEOPLE:

4 bell peppers (in different colors)

FOR THE DRESSING:

2 garlic cloves
1 tablespoon fresh thyme leaves
6 tablespoons olive oil
3 tablespoons balsamic vinegar
1 tablespoon runny honey
salt, black pepper
2 tablespoons pine nuts

WHAT OTHER antipasti CAN I SERVE?

Here are some ideas: • sundried tomatoes on toast • goat's cheese on crackers • salami slices • prosciutto (ham) • figs wrapped in bacon and grilled • marinated mushrooms • shrimps in garlic and lemon sauce • bruschetta (toast with tomato and garlic spread) • spicy olives • fried calamari

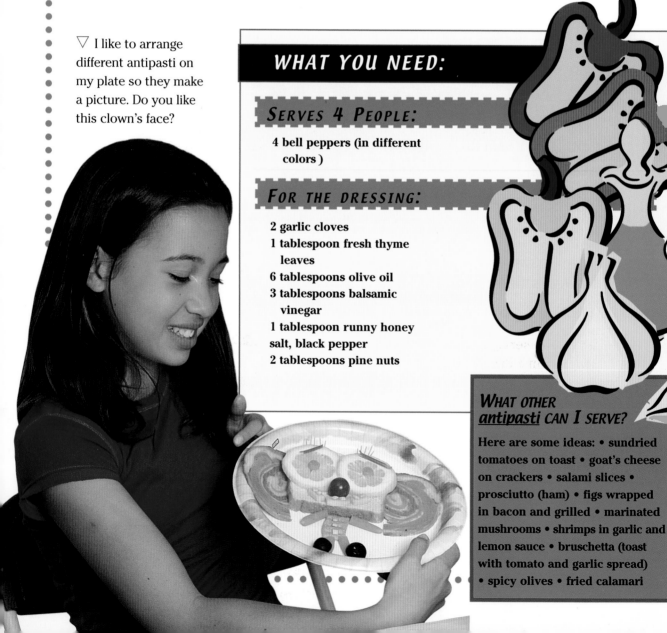

1 Heat the oven to 480°F. Halve the bell peppers lengthways. Cut out the stalks and the white skins, and scrape out the seeds.

2 Wash the pepper halves and place them with the round side up on the baking tray. Bake them in the oven for 10–15 minutes, until the skin goes black and blisters.

3 Take the tray out of the oven and cover it with a damp kitchen cloth. Allow to cool until you can touch the peppers without burning yourself.

4 With a knife, pull off the burned skin and throw it away. (It doesn't matter if some bits don't come off.) Cut the peppers into 1-inch-wide strips.

5 Peel and crush the garlic into a small bowl. Add the thyme, olive oil, vinegar, honey, salt, and pepper. Stir everything well to combine.

6 Arrange the pepper strips on a serving platter. Drizzle over the marinade. Cover with plastic wrap and allow to stand for at least 4 hours.

7 Just before serving, roast the pine nuts in a dry skillet *(see page 19)* until they are golden brown. Sprinkle them over the peppers.

let's make...
PIZZA MARGHERITA

Is this the Number One popular food in the world? I think so. And where does it come from? Italy! There are many, many different toppings for a pizza… Here is one.

WHAT YOU NEED:

SERVES 4 PEOPLE:

1 ounce fresh yeast	4 tablespoons
1 pinch sugar	olive oil
1 lb flour	1 teaspoon salt

FOR THE TOPPING:

1 large can peeled tomatoes	4 tablespoons
½ lb mozzarella	olive oil
salt, black pepper	1 to 2 handfuls
4 tablespoons grated	fresh basil
Parmesan cheese	

PLUS:

olive oil for the baking dish

△ Pizza in the park—there is nothing better. We do pizza parties—everyone invents their own topping. Then we judge the result. Some crazy, but tasty, ideas are tomatoes, honey, and cheese; or Mexican chocolate and chicken!

MAKE IT *American*

In Italy, we like pizza with a thin crispy crust. But you can make this an American pizza: double the ingredients for the base, roll it out thickly, and then bake it at 400°F for about 15 minutes.

1 Crumble the yeast into a bowl. Stir in 5 tablespoons lukewarm water and the sugar. Stir in 3 tablespoons flour. Cover with a cloth and allow to rest in a warm place for 20 minutes.

2 Add the rest of the flour, the olive oil, salt, and about ¾ cup lukewarm water. Knead together until you have a smooth dough. Cover with a cloth and stand in a warm spot for another 1 hour.

3 Heat the oven to 480°F. Brush four pizza molds (8 inches diameter) with oil. Divide the dough in fourths. Roll out each portion to a flat round disk. Put them into the pizza molds.

4 Drain the tomatoes in a sieve. Spread them over the pizza bases and squash them with a fork. Leave a 1-inch edge uncovered all round.

5 Cut the mozzarella into thin slices and place them on the pizzas. Season with salt and pepper. Sprinkle with the Parmesan and drizzle with a little olive oil.

6 Bake the pizzas, one after another, on the lowest shelf in the oven for about 8–10 minutes. Garnish with basil leaves and serve.

let's make...
TIRAMISU

This super dessert was invented only about fifty years ago in the Veneto region, but today everyone thinks it's the most classic and Italian of all possible desserts.

▽ Tiramisu means "pick-me-up." When I'm down in the dumps, all I need is a spoonful of this divine dessert, and I feel on top of the world.

WHAT YOU NEED:

SERVES 4 PEOPLE (OR MAYBE 3):

2 fresh egg yolks
2 tablespoons sugar
½ lb mascarpone cheese
1 teaspoon grated zest of an untreated lemon
½ cup hot chocolate
4 ounces ladyfinger cookies
1 tablespoon cocoa powder

WHAT'S THIS: <u>mascarpone?</u>

Mascarpone is a triple-cream cheese. It's made from the milk of cows that have been fed a special diet. If you cannot find any mascarpone in the stores, use ricotta cheese or cottage cheese instead. Whip it with a fork until it is very smooth.

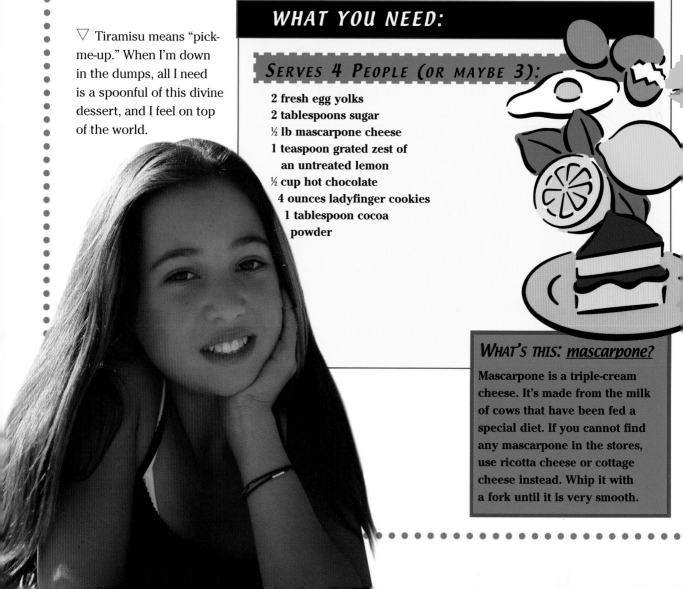

1 Put the egg yolks, the sugar, and 4 tablespoons of hot water into a bowl. Beat everything with a handheld whisk for about 5 minutes, or until it is thick and creamy.

2 Add the mascarpone cheese to the egg mixture, a spoonful at a time. Stir it in with a fork. Stir in the lemon zest. Put the chocolate into a shallow dish.

4 Spread the cookies with half the mascarpone cheese. Smooth the layer with the back of a spoon. Dip the remaining cookies in the chocolate, then place them on top of the cheese layer. Spread these cookies with the remaining mascarpone and smooth everything again so the top is even.

3 Dip half the ladyfinger cookies in the chocolate. Line the base of a shallow dish with the cookies.

5 Cover the tiramisu with a clean cloth or plastic wrap. Chill in the fridge for at least 3 hours. Just before serving, dust the dessert with cocoa powder.

Look it up
ITALY

al dente a description for how pasta is cooked; it still has "bite," and is neither too hard nor too soggy

antipasti Italian starters; many different small nibbles are counted as antipasti, from marinated peppers, mushrooms, or eggplant to salami or ham slices

La Befana an old woman from Italian legend; she is said to come with her broom and distribute gifts and candies on January 6

bolognese or alla bolognese: a meat sauce in the style typical of Bologna, a town in northern Italy

confetti (1) small paper pieces thrown at weddings; (2) an Italian candy: sugar-coated almonds that are given as favors for special events

mascarpone a triple-cream cheese from Lombardy, white and easy to spread; an important ingredient in tiramisu

Parmesan a hard cheese from Parma, in northern Italy; it is often grated over pasta dishes at the table

pancetta an Italian fatty bacon, cured and spiced, and usually rolled

pesto a cold pasta sauce made from basil leaves, garlic, oil, pine nuts, and Pecorino cheese

prosciutto a North Italian dry-cured ham; the best known is Parma ham; it is usually cut into very thin slices

riposo the Italian word for a siesta, a period of rest after lunch during which shops are closed

saltimbocca literally: leap-in-the-mouth; an Italian dish made from veal cutlets; it is fried with prosciutto and sage leaves

tiramisu literally: pick-me-up; an Italian dessert, made from mascarpone, cocoa or coffee, and ladyfinger cookies

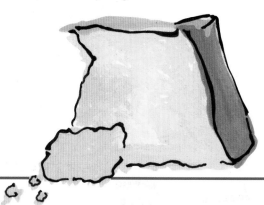

Find out more
ITALY

Books to read

Sansone, Emma, and Woolley, Kim.
Getting to Know: Italy and Italian.
Barrons Educational Series, 1993.

Behnke, Alison.
Italy in Pictures.
Visual Geography, Lerner Publications,
revised edition 2002.

Nickles, Greg.
**Italy — The people (Lands, Peoples, and
Cultures).**
Crabtree Publishing Company, 2001.

Petersen, Christine and David.
Italy.
Children's Press, CT, 2002.

Web sites to check out

www.enit.it
The official Italian tourist board Web site

www.www.italymag.co.uk
A site for all those who love Italy, with
food, drink, fashion, sports, history, art,
gardens, places to see, people gossip

**www3.nationalgeographic.com/places/
countries/country_italy.html**
The National Geographic's site about
Italy, with information about history,
travel, flags, photographs

www.italianfoodforever.com
All about Italian food and drink, including
recipes, articles, and a monthly newsletter

www.angelfire.com/il2/sito/bambini.html
Information for children, with picture
dictionaries, phrases, stories, and music

**http://italian.about.com/library/children/
blchildrenhome.htm**
Online language-learning site for children

Index
ITALY